Little Pebble™

Healthy Me

I KEEP CLEAN

by Martha E. H. Rustad

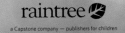

raintree

a Capstone company — publishers for children

Raintree is an imprint of Capstone Global Library Limited, a company incorporated in England and Wales having its registered office at 264 Banbury Road, Oxford, OX2 7DY – Registered company number: 6695582

www.raintree.co.uk
myorders@raintree.co.uk

Edited by Shelly Lyons
Designed by Juliette Peters
Picture research by Jo Miller
Production by Tori Abraham

ISBN 978 1 4747 3486 8
20 19 18 17 16
10 9 8 7 6 5 4 3 2 1

British Library Cataloguing in Publication Data
A full catalogue record for this book is available from the British Library.

Acknowledgements
Images by Capstone Studio: Karon Dubke
Photo Styling: Sarah Schuette and Marcy Morin

Printed and bound in China.

Contents

Get clean

Football is hard work.

I am hot and sweaty.

It is time to get clean.

I need a shower or bath.

Warm water feels good.

I have a bath or shower

every other day.

Soap cleans my skin.

My armpits need washing.

I clean my feet too.

I wash my whole body.

I wash my hair.

I scrub my scalp.

I rinse off the bubbles.

I find a clean towel.

It helps me get dry.

I dry between my toes.

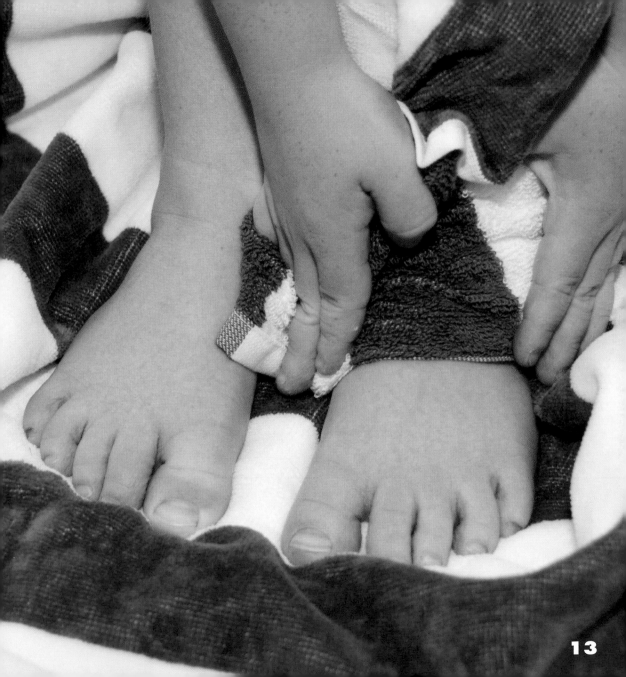

Clean clothes

I put on clean clothes.

They keep my body clean.

My shoes get smelly.

I let them air outside.

Sweaty feet make

smelly shoes!

Wash hands

I use the toilet.

Then I wash my hands.

I stop germs from spreading.

I keep clean.
A clean me
is a healthy me!

Glossary

germs tiny organisms that sometimes cause illness

rinse to wash something with clean water to get rid of soap

scalp the skin on your head; hair grows out of your scalp

shampoo a thick liquid that cleans your hair

sweaty wet with a liquid from your body; sweat helps cool your body; sweat sometimes smells bad

Find out more

Books

Keeping Clean (Let's Read and Talk About), Honor Head
(Franklin Watts, 2014)

Keeping Clean (Looking After Me), Liz Grogerly
(Wayland, 2012)

Keeping Clean (Take Care of Yourself!), Sian Smith
(Raintree, 2013)

Websites

kidshealth.org/en/kids/stay-healthy/
Tips on keeping fit and having fun.

www.bbc.co.uk/guides/zxvkd2p
A video shows you how to stay healthy.

Comprehension questions

1. When washing your hair, what do you need to rinse?

2. Why is it important to wash your hands after using the toilet?

3. When you wash, you get rid of germs. What are germs?

Index